She Plays Soccer

By Trudy Becker

level 2 little blue readers

www.littlebluehousebooks.com

Little Blue House is distributed by North Star Editions:
sales@northstareditions.com | 888-417-0195

Produced for Little Blue House by Red Line Editorial.

Photographs ©: iStockphoto, cover, 4, 7, 11, 12, 16, 19, 21, 23, 24 (top left), 24 (top right), 24 (bottom left), 24 (bottom right); Shutterstock Images, 9 (top), 9 (bottom), 15

Library of Congress Control Number: 2022910478

ISBN
978-1-64619-710-1 (hardcover)
978-1-64619-742-2 (paperback)
978-1-64619-802-3 (ebook pdf)
978-1-64619-774-3 (hosted ebook)

Printed in the United States of America
Mankato, MN
012023

About the Author

Trudy Becker lives in Minneapolis, Minnesota. She likes exploring new places and loves anything involving books.

Table of Contents

Getting Ready

I play soccer.

I love game days.

I get ready to play.

I put on my uniform.

I wear shorts and a jersey.

I match my team.

I put on my shin guards and socks.

They keep my legs safe.

I put on my cleats.

They help me run fast.

I fill my water bottle and pick up my soccer ball. I put everything in my bag.

soccer ball

water bottle

On the Field

Games happen on the soccer field.

The field has white lines on it.

There is a big goal at each end.

Fans watch from the side of the field.

They cheer for the players.

fans

In the Game

I listen for the whistle.

It blows to start each game.

I keep my hands away.

They can't touch the ball.

I dribble the ball down the field.

I kick the ball with my right foot.

Then I use my left foot.

dribble

Sometimes I can't take
a shot.

So, I look around the field.

I pass the ball.

Other times, I shoot the
ball toward the goal.

I kick it hard.

I score!

I love soccer.

Glossary

dribble

jersey

goal

soccer ball

Index